My Science Library

Eating and the Digestive System

by Julie K. Lundgren

Science Content Editor:
Shirley Duke

Rourke
Educational Media

rourkeeducationalmedia.com

Teacher Notes available at
rem4teachers.com

Science Content Editor: Shirley Duke holds a bachelor's degree in biology and a master's degree in education from Austin College in Sherman, Texas. She taught science in Texas at all levels for twenty-five years before starting to write for children. Her science books include *You Can't Wear These Genes, Infections, Infestations, and Diseases, Enterprise STEM, Forces and Motion at Work, Environmental Disasters,* and *Gases.* She continues writing science books and also works as a science content editor.

www.rourkeeducationalmedia.com

Photo credits: Cover © Khoroshunova Olga, stefbennett, John L. Absher; Pages 2/3 © Oguz Aral; Pages 4/5 © Robyn Mackenzie, Dmitry Kalinovsky, SeDmi, USDA, Monkey Business Images; Pages 6/7 © Katarzyna Mazurowska, Leah-Anne Thompson; Pages 8/9 © Monkey Business Images, ARENA Creative, Alexander Trinitatov; Pages 10/11 © Oguz Aral, Edyta Pawlowska; Pages 12/13 © Oguz Aral, Neeila; Pages 14/15 © photosync, sandracws; Pages 16/17 © mark, Tony Campbell; Pages 18/19 © stefbennett, Eric Isselée, Arto Hakola; Pages 20/21 © Sters, kostudio, AI vision, Konjushenko Vladimir, Studio 37

Editor: Kelli Hicks

My Science Library series produced by Blue Door Publishing, Florida for Rourke Educational Media.

Library of Congress PCN Data

Lundgren, Julie K.
 Eating and the Digestive System / Julie K. Lundgren.
    p. cm. -- (My Science Library)
 ISBN 978-1-61810-101-3 (Hard cover) (alk. paper)
 ISBN 978-1-61810-234-8 (Soft cover)
 Library of Congress Control Number: 2012930301

Rourke Educational Media
Printed in the United States of America,
North Mankato, Minnesota

rourkeeducationalmedia.com

customerservice@rourkeeducationalmedia.com • PO Box 643328 Vero Beach, Florida 32964

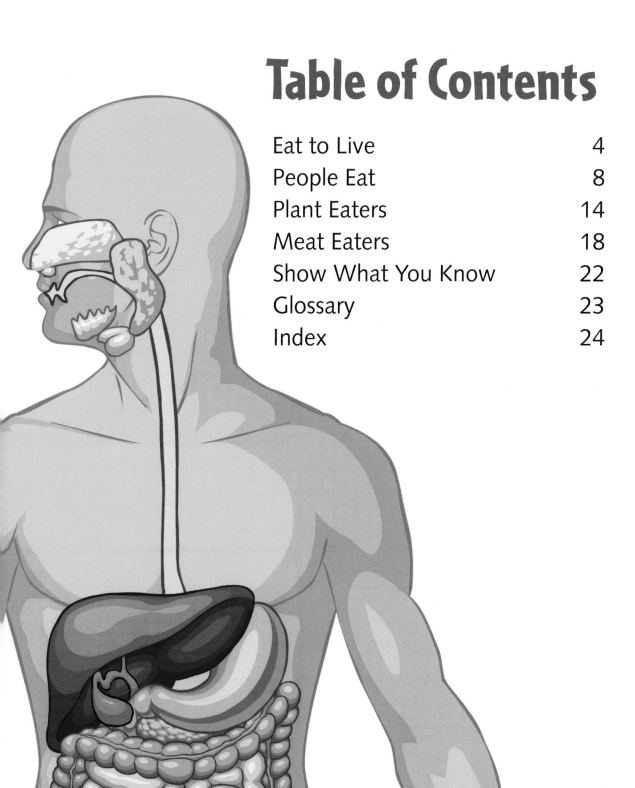

Table of Contents

Eat to Live

Animals and people need to eat to fuel their bodies. Healthy food helps bodies grow, repair themselves, and do the work of living. Eating passes energy along from the food item to the eater.

Meat, eggs, and fish contain protein, needed for building muscle.

A Healthy Plate

A balanced diet with lots of fruits and vegetables helps people stay healthy. What about dessert? Eat sweets only occasionally and in small amounts. A growing body needs healthy food.

Dairy foods like milk, yogurt, and cheese help keep our bones and teeth strong.

Whole grains like oats, wheat, and brown rice supply long-lasting energy.

The digestive system changes food to a form the body can use as fuel. The digestive system is a pathway through the body with stops along the way, like a bus route. Food enters, breaks down, and then the wastes exit along this route.

Glug, Glug, Glug

Water helps your body break down food during digestion. After sports, drink water to feel refreshed.

Active bodies need food for fuel.

People Eat

Each part of the digestive system has a purpose. In people, food enters through the mouth. Teeth begin breaking down food by biting and chewing. Our **saliva**, or spit, moistens dry food and contains enzymes that begin the digestive process. Enzymes and other ingredients in saliva help kill bacteria that may cause illness and tooth decay.

Taking small bites and chewing carefully aids digestion.

Without saliva, our tongues would not be able to taste. Swallowing sends chewed food on its path to the stomach through a long tube called the esophagus.

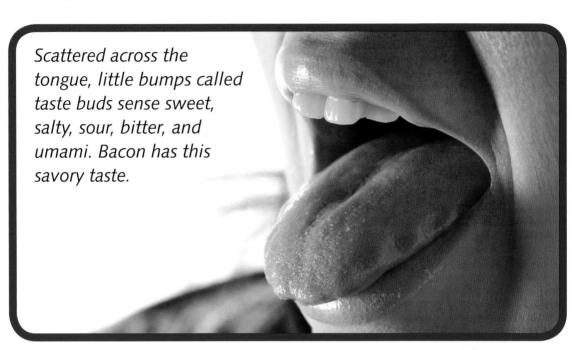

Scattered across the tongue, little bumps called taste buds sense sweet, salty, sour, bitter, and umami. Bacon has this savory taste.

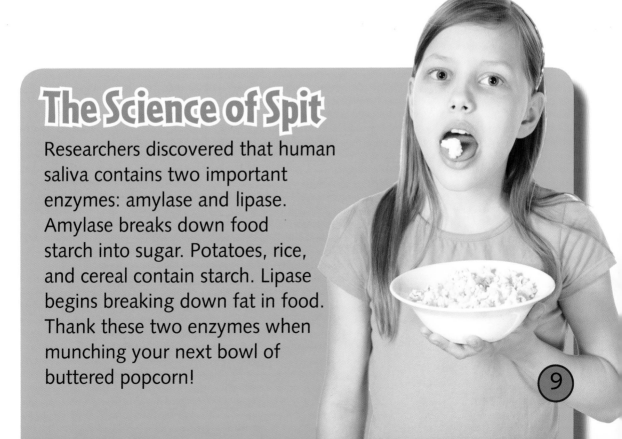

The Science of Spit

Researchers discovered that human saliva contains two important enzymes: amylase and lipase. Amylase breaks down food starch into sugar. Potatoes, rice, and cereal contain starch. Lipase begins breaking down fat in food. Thank these two enzymes when munching your next bowl of buttered popcorn!

The stomach has two important jobs. First, it acts as a place to store food. It allows us to eat a whole meal and then go do something besides eat for several hours at a time.

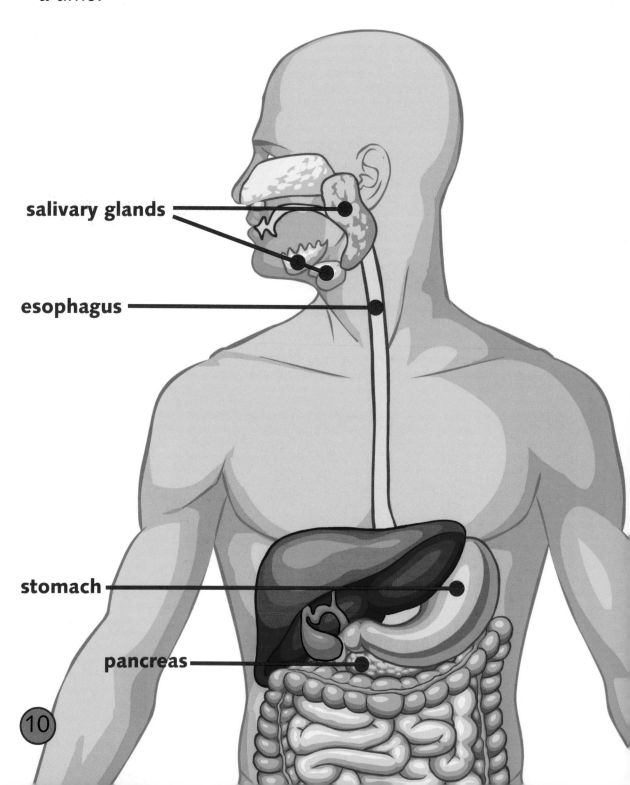

salivary glands

esophagus

stomach

pancreas

Second, the stomach continues the food breakdown started in the mouth. It contains **acid** and its walls have muscles. These muscles cause the stomach to churn the food and acid until it turns into a liquid paste, like a chunky malt. After several hours, most of the food moves on to the small **intestine**.

Why do stomachs growl?

As the stomach moves and grooves, it squeezes liquids and gas bubbles, too. Having food inside quiets the sound. We hear these sounds more easily on an empty stomach.

The stomach stretches to hold an entire meal, and then it gets smaller as it slowly empties.

The small intestine is a long, soft, hollow tube. It snakes back and forth in your lower **abdomen**. Your **pancreas** provides enzymes and other digestive aids to the small intestine to finish breaking down fats and protein. Through the intestine's thin, complex walls, tiny molecules of digested food and water pass to the bloodstream.

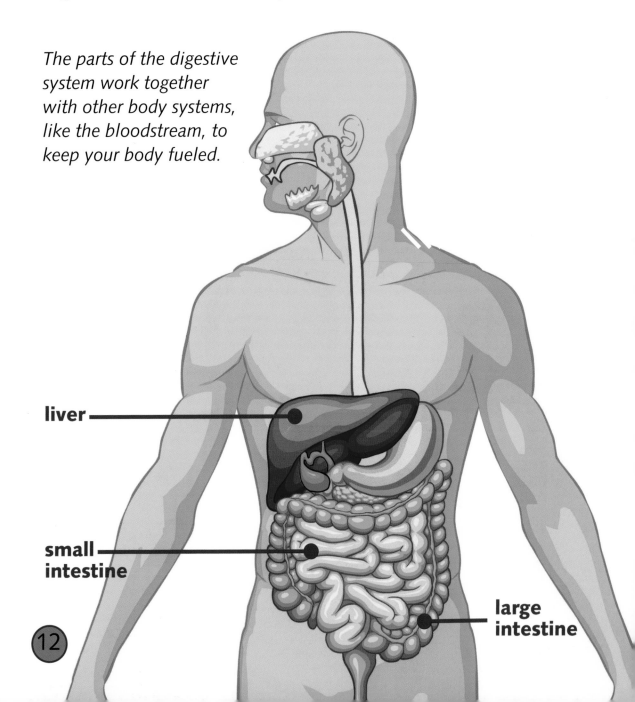

The parts of the digestive system work together with other body systems, like the bloodstream, to keep your body fueled.

liver

small intestine

large intestine

Bile from your liver helps digest fats so they can move into the blood. The bloodstream carries the food molecules to all parts of the body. Next, undigested food, or waste, moves from the small intestine to the large intestine and exits the body.

Fact Snack

If laid out straight, the small intestine of an average adult would stretch 22 feet (6.7 meters) long. The large intestine is shorter than the small intestine, but much wider.

Down Then Up

Sometimes, when you're feeling sick, dizzy, or nervous, you throw up. That chunky malt of partly digested food, stomach acid, and sour bile shoots out through your mouth. That's the stomach getting rid of food fast. Everyone tosses their cookies once in awhile. If you throw up, try to relax. Rinse out your mouth to get rid of the bad taste, and then rest. Sip a little water and wait for the feeling to pass.

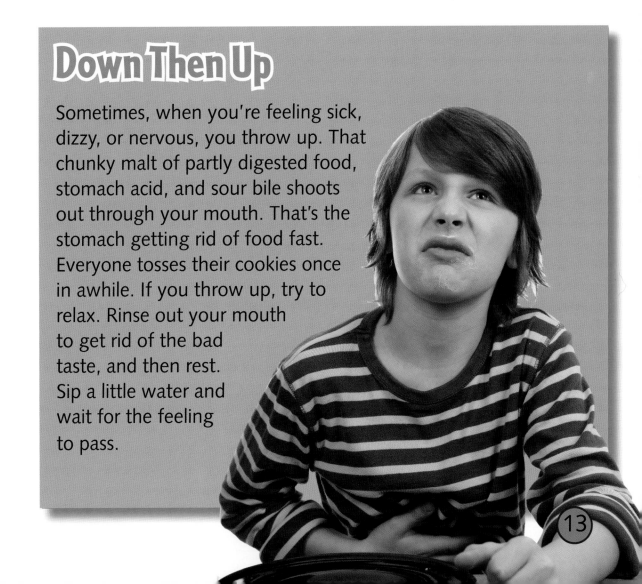

Plant Eaters

Animal digestive systems have many of the same parts as human systems. Depending on the animal, some parts have changed over time to better digest the foods they eat. These adaptations help animals survive.

Plant eaters, or herbivores, eat tough or woody stems, leaves, grasses, and other plant parts. Because these materials are harder to break down, plants take longer to digest than meat.

Creative Juices

Animals have developed special ways to use their saliva, other than digestion. Certain kinds of birds called swifts use their saliva as glue for building nests. Cobras and some other venomous snakes have poison in their saliva to inject into and kill or stun their prey.

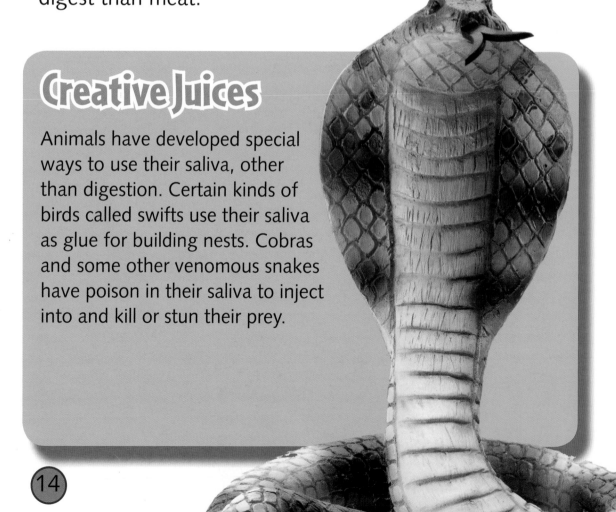

Pandas chomp bamboo.

Some kinds of herbivores have stomachs with several rooms or separate spaces. Giraffes, cows, and some other herbivores chew their **cud**. They bring up a ball of partly digested food from the first part of the stomach and chew it again. Herbivores also have very long small intestines to give their bodies time to take up all possible **nutrients**.

Birds have no teeth for chewing. Instead many have a **crop**, a special pocket made of muscle for grinding and storing food. This pocket is a stop on the way to the stomach. Even birds that eat meat can have crops.

Hawks and many other birds gobble as much food as they can very quickly, before another animal can steal their meal. They store and begin to digest the food in their crops.

crop

crop

Bird crops often have grains of sand or small rocks inside to help grind food.

Meat Eaters

Meat digests more easily than plants. Still, carnivores have adaptations for eating and digesting meat. Wolves, coyotes, and cats have special teeth called **canines** shaped for gripping and killing prey. The long, sharp canine teeth sit on either side of the top and bottom front teeth. Behind each canine lies a row of slicing teeth, the **carnassials**. As a carnivore chews, the top and bottom rows of carnassial teeth come together like scissor blades.

Birds of prey have powerful feet for catching and holding prey and hooked beaks for tearing food. Since they do not have teeth, they use these tools to strip off pieces of meat and swallow them whole.

People have knives and forks, but animals use built-in silverware. This is especially important for owls, who do not have crops.

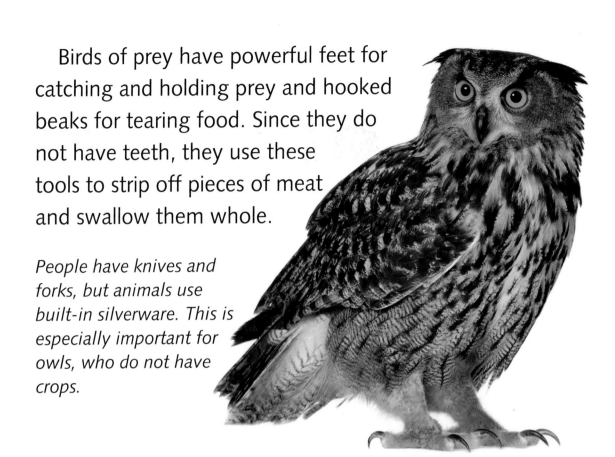

Dining on the Dead

Carrion can contain millions of tiny bacteria. Scavengers have strong stomach acid that kills bacteria or germs in the rotting meat. The turkey vulture has another adaptation for eating carrion. It has a featherless head for easy clean up after feasting on the dead.

Animals that eat both plants and animals have a combination of the adaptations found in herbivores and carnivores. Humans do not chew cud, but we do have front teeth shaped for biting and flat, back teeth for grinding our food. Digestive systems have adaptations to perfectly suit every diet.

Sink your teeth into this quiz!

In the photos below, which mouths eat meat? Which eats plants? Whoa! Which mouth needs some serious brushing?

Fact Snack

A beaver's front teeth never stop growing. It must bite, gnaw, and nibble every day to keep them short.

The Daily Grind

Compare your teeth to dog, cat, or horse teeth. How are they the same? How are they different?

Show What You Know

1. What is the purpose of the small intestine?

2. What adaptations do herbivores have to help them digest their food?

3. What special ways do birds digest food?

Glossary

abdomen (AB-duh-muhn): in people, the section of the body below the chest where the main parts of the digestive system are located

acid (ASS-ihd): a substance that causes the breakdown of things it touches

canines (KAY-nynez): the long, sharp, pointed teeth of carnivores that grip and kill prey

carnassials (kar-NASS-ee-uhlz): in meat eaters, the rows of slicing teeth behind the canine teeth

crop (KROP): in some birds, a pouch between the mouth and the stomach where food is ground

cud (KUHD): a ball of partly digested food that certain herbivores regularly bring up from their stomach for chewing again

intestine (in-TESS-tin): the lower part of the digestive system in animals and people, where nutrients and water are absorbed, including the small and large intestine

nutrients (NOO-tree-uhnts): things foods contain that are needed for healthy growth, like vitamins and minerals

pancreas (PAN-kree-uhss): an organ in the digestive system that sends enzymes and other ingredients to the small intestine to break down fats and protein

saliva (suh-LYE-vuh): spit, made by the mouth to aid digestion and the sense of taste

Index

Websites to Visit

www.ecokids.ca/pub/kids_home.cfm

www.nhptv.org/NatureWorks/nwep10b.htm

www.vtaide.com/png/foodchains.htm

About the Author

Julie K. Lundgren has written more than 40 nonfiction books for children. She gets a kick out of sharing juicy facts about science, nature, and animals, especially if they are slightly disgusting! Through her work, she hopes kids will learn that Earth is an amazing place and young people can make a big difference in keeping our planet healthy. She lives in Minnesota with her family.

Ask The Author!
www.rem4students.com